Elizabeth and Her Court

LIFE IN ELIZABETHAN ENGLAND

Elizabeth and Her Court

KATHRYN HINDS

SEVERNA PARK HIGH SCHOOL

MARSHALL CAVENDISH BENCHMARK NEW YORK

To Tyra

The author and publisher specially wish to thank Dr. Megan Lynn Isaac,
former associate professor of Renaissance Literature at Youngstown State University, Ohio,
for her invaluable help in reviewing the manuscript.

MARSHALL CAVENDISH BENCHMARK 99 WHITE PLAINS ROAD TARRYTOWN, NEW YORK 10591-9001
www.marshallcavendish.us Text copyright © 2008 by Marshall Cavendish Corporation All rights reserved. No part of
this book may be reproduced or utilized in any form or by any means electronic or mechanical including photocopying,
recording, or by any information storage and retrieval system, without permission from the copyright holders. All Internet
sites were available and accurate when this book was sent to press. LIBRARY OF CONGRESS CATALOGING-IN-PUBLICATION
DATA Hinds, Kathryn, 1962- Elizabeth and her court / by Kathryn Hinds. p. cm. — (Life in Elizabethan England)
Summary: "A social history of Elizabethan England, focusing on life in the upper echelons of society during the famous
monarch's reign: 1558-1603"—Provided by publisher. Includes bibliographical references and index. ISBN-13: 978-0-
7614-2542-7 1. Elizabeth I, Queen of England, 1533-1603—Relations with courts and courtiers—Juvenile literature. 2.
Great Britain—Court and courtiers—History—16th century—Juvenile literature. 3. Great Britain—Court and courtiers—
Social life and customs—16th century—Juvenile literature. 4. Great Britain—History—Elizabeth, 1558-1603—Juvenile
literature. I. Title. DA355.H56 2007 942.05′5092—dc22 2006029587

EDITOR: Joyce Stanton   PUBLISHER: Michelle Bisson
ART DIRECTOR: Anahid Hamparian   SERIES DESIGNER: Michael Nelson

Printed in Malaysia
135642

front cover: Shakespeare reads to Queen Elizabeth in a scene imagined by nineteenth-century artist John James Chalon.
half-title page: A portrait of a little girl by Isaac Oliver, one of Elizabeth's favorite painters.
title page: A group of aristocratic men, perhaps members of Elizabeth's Privy Council, relax with a game of cards in this
   painting from around 1570.
back cover: Lady Katherine Seymour holds her young son in this miniature by Levina Teerlinc, who was a lady-in-waiting as
   well as a court artist.

CONTENTS

Nicholas Hilliard, a famous Elizabethan artist, painted
this miniature portrait of a young man in a rose garden.

About Elizabethan England

IT WAS A GOLDEN AGE: A TIME OF POETRY, THEATER, AND SONG; intrigue, adventure, and exploration; faith, intellect, and passion; trials, triumphs, and splendor. The reign of Elizabeth I, from 1558 to 1603, was like no other era of English history. Under Elizabeth's leadership, England began the journey from small, isolated, poor island nation to thriving world power. Under the poets and playwrights of Elizabeth's time—above all, William Shakespeare—the English language reached new heights, and a powerful body of literature was created, one that still delights and inspires us. Elizabeth invited and influenced other forms of creativity as well, and her rule left indelible marks not only in the arts but in politics, religion, and society. The glories—and the troubles—of her reign are all part of the heritage shared by England and its former colonies.

This series of books looks at the Elizabethan age with a focus on its people and their everyday lives, whether they were at the top of society, the bottom, or somewhere in the middle. We will see how they worked, where they lived, how they related to one another, how they relaxed and celebrated special occasions, how they coped with life's hardships. In this volume we will meet the nobility of England and the gentlemen and ladies of Elizabeth's court—and of course, the glorious queen herself. These people had many of the same joys and sorrows, hopes and fears that we do. They were poised at the beginning of the modern age, but still their world was very different from ours. Forget about telephones, computers, cars, and televisions, and step back in time. . . . Welcome to life in Elizabethan England!

One Mistress and No Master

I am already bound unto a husband, which is the kingdom of England . . .
everyone of you, and as many as are English,
are my children and kinsfolks.
— ELIZABETH I, HER FIRST SPEECH TO PARLIAMENT

ELIZABETH TUDOR WAS TWENTY-FIVE YEARS OLD when she became queen of England in 1558. She was the last surviving child of Henry VIII, who had divorced his first wife to marry Elizabeth's mother, Anne Boleyn. But the marriage did not turn out as Henry had hoped, and ended with him ordering Anne beheaded for treason. The death of her mother made a fearful impression on Elizabeth, who was nearing age three at the time. When she was eight, Henry had another of his wives executed. Elizabeth declared then that she would never marry, and events in the following years only increased her determination not to let her fate be controlled by a man, or by anyone else.

When Henry married Anne Boleyn, he broke from the Catholic Church and founded the Church of England, a Protestant church with himself at its head. As king after him, his young son Edward

Opposite: Elizabeth at the age of thirteen, a year before Henry VIII's death. She was third in line for her father's throne.

9

This 1910 painting shows Queen Mary arriving in London at the time of her coronation in 1553, attended by her half sister Princess Elizabeth (in red).

strengthened English Protestantism. Edward was succeeded by his half sister Mary, a Catholic. She declared England a Catholic country once more. Influenced by her husband, King Philip II of Spain, she persecuted many Protestants who refused to change their faith. These were bad years for the majority of English people, who by now had embraced Protestantism. They were bad years, too, for Mary's half sister Elizabeth, who was raised in the Protestant faith. To keep peace with Mary, she followed at least the outward forms of Catholicism, but Mary still suspected her religious convictions. At one point she had Elizabeth arrested and imprisoned in the Tower of London on suspicion of treason. While there, Elizabeth lived in constant fear that she would meet her mother's fate. For the rest of her life afterward, she gave thanks to God that she was finally declared innocent and released.

When Mary died and Elizabeth came to the throne, most of England rejoiced. And everyone waited to see what she would do about the country's religious situation. Elizabeth knew that a large minority of her people were sincerely devoted to the Catholic faith, and she did not want to see England torn by religious wars, as happened in some parts of Europe. Yet she and other Protestants were suspicious of Catholic loyalty to the pope—a foreign power, as far as they were concerned. So, early in her reign, Elizabeth forged a settlement that made Protestantism the official faith. At the same time, she made sure that the Church of England kept some Catholic practices, and she allowed Catholics limited freedom of religion. Many English were dissatisfied with the compromise, and many foreigners were outraged—particularly the rulers of the powerful Catholic countries across the English Channel.

Already isolated by geography, England became isolated by religion. And in addition to divisions within the nation and enemies without, there were serious financial problems, for Queen Mary had run up a large national debt. It would take a remarkable ruler to lead England to unity, security, and prosperity. Fortunately, Elizabeth was just such a ruler.

MARRIED TO ENGLAND

"I know I have the body but of a weak and feeble woman; but I have the heart and stomach [spirit] of a king, and of a king of England too." These were Elizabeth's proud words to her troops in 1588, when the nation was preparing to repel an invasion by Spain. She had always been aware that most Europeans didn't believe a woman had the ability to be a ruler. But she had proven to the English over and over again that she was the equal of any king—and the superior of many. "Let tyrants fear," she said in this same speech; "I have placed my chief strength and safeguard in the loyal hearts and good-will of my subjects." Indeed, she saw them as more than just her subjects; they were "my faithful and loving people."

In Elizabeth's time, it was believed that the best service a queen could do her country was to marry, so that her rule could be guided by a man, and have sons, so that there would be a king to come after her. But Elizabeth refused to follow this path, confident that on her own she was better suited than anyone else to rule her nation. She often declared that she could not take a husband because she was already married to England. Sometimes she did appear to consider

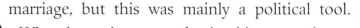

marriage, but this was mainly a political tool. When her suitors were foreign kings or princes, she could use marriage negotiations as a way to play one nation off against another. Even when it came to men she seemed to be genuinely fond of, she knew that if she had a husband, she would lose much of her authority to him. As she once proclaimed to her friend Robert Dudley, the Earl of Leicester, "I will have here but one mistress and no master."

Over the years, Elizabeth built up the idea of her marriage to England, constantly expressing her devotion to her people. The people loved it. They praised her as Good Queen Bess, the Virgin Queen, Eliza Triumphant, and Gloriana, the poet Edmund Spenser's "Faerie Queene." They compared her to goddesses and heroines from the Bible, classical mythology, and history. Diana, the virgin moon goddess of ancient Rome, was a favorite comparison, as in these lines by Spenser:

Elizabeth owned around three thousand gowns. She favored relatively simple, dark clothing when she was busy working on government business. For portraits and public appearances, however, she dressed with as much splendor as possible.

. . . O Goddesse heavenly bright,
Mirrour of grace and Majestie divine,
Great Lady of the greatest Isle, whose light
Like Phoebus lampe throughout the world doth shine . . .

Others expressed their love for their ruler more simply: "We did nothing but talk of what an admirable Queen she was," wrote one young man after hearing Elizabeth address a London crowd. As the historian John Hayward wrote in the early 1600s, "If ever any person had either the gift or the style to win the hearts of people, it was this queen."

LEADING THE NATION

It was not just the power of Elizabeth's personality that made her a well-loved ruler. She also had great intelligence, courage, and a real talent for government. She was a gifted public speaker and a fine actor as well, able to play whatever role worked to her advantage. She could be supremely dignified, cold and calculating, flirtatious, tender, intellectual, lighthearted, indecisive, fiercely determined—whatever the situation called for. Her capacity for hard work was legendary, as was her self-discipline. She kept herself well informed of conditions in her own kingdom and abroad. One of her councillors wrote, "There was never so wise woman born as Queen Elizabeth, for she spake and understood all languages, knew all estates and dispositions and princes, and particularly was so expert in the knowledge of her own realm as no counsellor she had could tell her what she knew not before."

Elizabeth was not an all-powerful ruler, however. She insisted on her authority, but she also had to answer to Parliament, which was made up of the hereditary nobles of the House of Lords and the elected members of the House of Commons. Parliament met only when the monarch summoned it, but its approval was required for any major changes in government policy. Moreover, English rulers could not impose taxes on the people without Parliament's consent, and taxation—money in general—was a serious issue for Elizabeth. Taxes were only levied for unusual expenses, such as defense costs in wartime. Otherwise the queen was expected to pay for almost every aspect of the national government out of her personal funds, the royal treasury. To build up the treasury, she relied on customs duties, loans, rents, sales of licenses and lands and offices, and plain old penny-pinching. She was notoriously frugal, something her advisers often complained about.

Country people often paid at least some of their taxes in the form of farm products.

As was expected of a ruler, Elizabeth kept a splendid court and spent substantial sums of money on pageantry; displays of royal wealth and power were important for her prestige both at home and abroad. Much of the luxury that surrounded her, however, was inherited, and she frequently received rich gifts from foreign ambassadors and from her own courtiers. Treasury funds went mainly for the upkeep of the royal palaces, the support of the household, the expenses of government departments, and the salaries of officials—only 1,200 of them, though, compared with France's 40,000; the English had no fondness for big government.

The military also had to be paid for out of the royal treasury. The treasury being small, so was the army: in addition to the two hundred men in the royal bodyguard, there were only a few hundred stationed to guard the southern coastline, where England was most vulnerable to invasion. If an invasion ever did come, the nation would count on local militias to defend it, though how effective they would be in battle was anyone's guess. One of the last things Elizabeth wanted was for war to come to her beloved country, and she exercised all her diplomatic skills to keep peace with the powerful and hostile nations of France and Spain. Diplomacy was supplemented by espionage—Elizabeth's councillor Francis Walsingham developed one of Europe's most efficient intelligence networks, with spies in ambassadors' households, foreign armies, and centers of business and government across the continent. These spies, too, were often paid with treasury funds—and they probably saved England from its enemies more than once.

ELIZABETH'S REALM

In his play *Richard II,* Shakespeare famously described England as

> This other Eden, demi-paradise,
> This fortress built by nature for herself
> Against infection and the hand of war,
> This happy breed of men, this little world,
> This precious stone set in the silver sea,
> Which serves it in the office of a wall,
> Or as a moat defensive to a house
> Against the envy of less happier lands;
> This blessèd plot, this earth, this realm, this England.

Shakespeare's description highlights the island nation's isolation thanks to the protecting sea. One of the effects of England's geographic situation was a particular sense of patriotism and pride in "Englishness" among the people—as well as a certain mistrust of foreigners and their ways. Elizabeth herself sympathized with this

NEIGHBORS, ALLIES, AND ENEMIES

Queen Mary and her husband, Philip II of Spain

England was not the only country on the island of Great Britain. To the north was the independent nation of Scotland, sometimes a troublesome neighbor because of its alliance with France. To the west was Wales, which had been united with England during King Henry VIII's reign but still maintained its own language and cultural identity. Further west, across the Irish Sea, lay Ireland, also subject to the English crown since Henry's reign. Like Wales, Ireland had its own language and culture; unlike Wales, it was (except for some of the English who had settled there) a Catholic country, and so was friendly to many of England's enemies.

France, across the English Channel from England, was one of the most powerful nations in sixteenth-century Europe. France and England had been enemies for hundreds of years, with English rulers claiming French territory as their own. Elizabeth's half sister Mary I, however, lost the last of England's holdings in France. During the course of Elizabeth's reign, relations with France became friendlier; for some time there was even talk of Elizabeth marrying a French prince.

Europe's other great power at this time was Spain, which was England's ally during Mary I's reign. Mary, a Catholic, married the Catholic king of Spain, Philip II. Philip considered it his duty to bring the Protestants of England and the Low Countries back to the Catholic Church. When Elizabeth made Protestantism England's official religion, relations between her country and Spain soured. They grew worse as England offered assistance to the Protestant cause in the Low Countries. Philip at last declared all-out war on Elizabeth, and England and Spain were mortal enemies for the rest of her reign.

viewpoint and emphasized that she was "descended by father and mother of mere English blood."

What were England and the English like during Elizabeth's time? In brief, the population was increasing, but still did not reach much above 4 million (Spain and France each had three to five times as many). Most of the people lived in country towns and villages, although more were moving to cities. The only major city, however, was London, with about 200,000 inhabitants by 1600. Literacy was on the rise, as it had been ever since the first printing press in England was established, in 1476—although few people learned to write, a great many were able to read. The middle class was growing, both in size and prosperity, but there was a widening gap between rich and poor. In spite of these changes in society, there remained a strong sense that every person was born into the rank God intended for them, and that each class owed special respect to the classes above.

The English of Elizabeth's time believed that there was an order to the universe, and that they had a part in it. This was probably one reason why they had a reputation for being stubborn and conservative. They were famous as a people who loved the law. Some might say they loved it too much—the courts were clogged with lawsuits thanks to incessant quarrels over legal rights to land use and other matters. The queen respected the law as much as her subjects. She knew, as a pamphlet published in the first year of her reign put it, that in a sense "it is not she that ruleth, but the laws." Her love of justice to all classes became legendary, leading Sir Walter Raleigh to say, "Queen Elizabeth would set the reason of a mean [humble] man before the authority of the greatest counsellor she had. She was Queen of the small as well as the great, and would hear their complaints."

2

Homes for the High and Mighty

Many of the splendid large rooms are embellished with masterly paintings,
writing tables of mother-of-pearl, and musical instruments,
of which Her Majesty is very fond.
⌐ PAUL HENTZNER, *A JOURNEY INTO ENGLAND IN THE YEAR 1598*

ELIZABETH'S REIGN BROUGHT PROSPERITY AND A HIGHER standard of living to many of her subjects, who enjoyed a new sense of energy and well-being. These qualities were expressed in a variety of ways, including an enthusiasm for home improvement—often on a grand scale. In what came to be known as "the Great Rebuilding," many members of the upper classes remodeled their hereditary castles and manor houses, or even pulled them down and replaced them with huge new homes of unprecedented luxury. Some even built their new houses in the shape of the letter E to flatter their queen. William Harrison described some of this building fervor in 1587:

The ancient manors and houses of our gentlemen are yet and for the most part of strong timber. . . . Howbeit such as

Opposite: Tapestries adorn the side walls of Hampton Court Palace's great hall. When Elizabeth stayed at the palace, all the members and guests of the court dined together here each day.

19

This stone manor house in southeastern England has changed little since it was built during the reign of Elizabeth I.

be lately builded, are commonly either of brick or hard stone, or both; their rooms large and comely [attractive]. . . . Those of the nobility are likewise wrought with brick and hard stone, as provision may best be made: but so magnificent and stately, as the basest house of a baron doth often match in our days with some honors of princes in old time.

ROYAL PALACES

Elizabeth herself was not much of a builder; there were other things she would rather spend her money on. She did make some improvements here and there—for example, adding a stone terrace to one palace, a banqueting house to another—but she was mainly content with what her father and grandfather had built, and what she had inherited from even earlier monarchs. Elizabeth owned fifty houses (some she rented out or eventually sold) and sixty castles. She spent little time in most of these, however: the royal palaces were the places she called home.

The queen's main residence in London was Whitehall Palace. When Elizabeth received visitors here, she often liked to stand in

Elizabeth and Her Court

front of a huge painting of Henry VIII—a reminder to everyone that she was the daughter and heir of a mighty king. It was Henry, in fact, who had enlarged Whitehall (with its outbuildings and grounds, it covered twenty-three acres) and beautified it with a magnificent collection of tapestries, paintings, and other decorations. In Elizabeth's time, Whitehall was one of Europe's largest palaces, with two thousand rooms.

Whitehall Palace and its portrait of Henry VIII no longer exist, but this copy of the portrait captures the imposing nature of Elizabeth's father.

The state rooms of Whitehall set the pattern for many other royal residences. There was a great hall, site of banquets and other festivities, which was semipublic. Off the great hall was the guard chamber, giving access to the presence chamber, which we might think of as the throne room. Next came the well-guarded privy chamber. This was where Elizabeth spent most of her time, working during the day and relaxing with card games, chess, and conversation in the evenings. In general, only the queen's close advisers and friends were admitted here. Even fewer people were welcomed in the next rooms, her private apartments, including her library and bedroom. When the queen was not in residence, however, visitors were allowed in to tour the rooms. A German traveler admired Elizabeth's bedroom in particular, with its bed "ingeniously composed of woods of different colours, with quilts of silk, velvet, gold, silver and embroidery." Another remarked on her bathtub, constructed so that "the water pours from oyster shells and different kinds of rock."

Nearly all the queen's palaces were situated

This manor house bedroom, visited by artist Joseph Nash in 1849, still had furnishings and richly carved wood paneling from the Elizabethan period, giving a hint of the even greater splendor that surrounded the queen.

beside the Thames River, making them easy for her to travel to in the royal barge, a splendid vessel rowed by twenty oarsmen. At Greenwich Palace (Elizabeth's birthplace), the presence chamber gave a stunning view of the river through its eighty feet of glass windows. This residence also featured an impressive riverside gatehouse, where Elizabeth welcomed distinguished visitors and watched naval displays on the Thames. Further upriver, west of London, lay Richmond Palace, built by Henry VII. The queen became very fond of Richmond as she grew older, referring to it as "a warm nest for my old age." Not only did it have a beautiful interior and gorgeous gardens, but Henry had provided it with indoor plumbing, bringing in pure water from a nearby spring. She was not so fond of Hampton Court Palace, however; as stunning as it was, it was full of bad memories of the time she almost died of smallpox there.

Windsor Castle, on the upper reaches of the Thames, was not as comfortable as Richmond, being drafty and hard to heat in the winter. But Elizabeth loved to be there in summertime. In the mornings she would take a brisk walk on the long stone terrace beneath her luxurious apartments. She could also stroll in the garden, with its

Elizabeth and Her Court

A view from the top of Windsor Castle's great round tower. The building in the center is St. George's Chapel, burial place of Henry VIII and several other English monarchs. Today, Windsor Castle is the official residence of Queen Elizabeth II.

paths and mazes; in bad weather, she walked in the ninety-foot-long indoor gallery. When she wanted to take more of a break from her royal duties, she enjoyed hunting in the great park that surrounded the castle. Part of Shakespeare's play *The Merry Wives of Windsor*, said to have been written at the queen's request, takes place in Windsor Great Park. The play was probably performed for Elizabeth, and toward the end there is a scene where fairies are called on to bless Windsor and its royal owner:

Search Windsor Castle, elves, within and out.
Strew good luck, oafs, on every sacred room,
That it may stand till the perpetual doom
In state as wholesome as in state 'tis fit,
Worthy the owner, and the owner it.

LIVING CONDITIONS

One of Elizabethan England's most ambitious builders was Elizabeth, Countess of Shrewsbury. She became known as Bess of Hardwick Hall, her splendid and enormous mansion, constructed between 1590 and 1603. Bess was the second-richest woman in

The front of Hardwick Hall, displaying "more glass than wall." Its builder was so proud of her home that she had her initials, *E.S.*, built into the decoration of the towers.

England (first was the queen), and she could afford to hire one of England's best architects. Her own lands, which included forests and stone quarries, provided most of the building materials. She also owned manufacturing facilities for iron and glass. This last item was an essential ingredient in setting Hardwick Hall and similar residences apart from the fortified manors and castles of old. Windows were no longer mere arrow slits: the style now was for tall glass windows, symmetrically arranged so that the exterior of the house would be "more glass than wall."

The setting of a house like Hardwick was carefully considered, and much energy went into landscaping. The expanses of windows let people indoors enjoy spacious views of the outdoors—and they wanted beautiful, dramatic, or interesting views. Gardening was a high art form; in addition to the kitchen gardens that produced food and medicinal herbs, there were ornamental gardens, meant to be both admired and enjoyed. In the early 1600s, the poet Amelia Lanyer fondly remembered the gardens and grounds belonging to a noblewoman with whom she had often stayed, recalling "each arbor, bank, each seat, each stately tree," and especially one particularly tall and beloved oak:

Where being seated, you might plainly see
Hills, vales, and woods, as if on bended knee . . .
All interlaced with brooks and crystal springs,
A prospect fit to please the eyes of kings.

Indoors, however, walls of windows and high ceilings made noble and royal homes difficult to heat with the fireplaces of the time—which is probably one reason why Elizabethan fashions featured high collars and layers of heavy fabrics. Similarly, the rich tapestries that bedecked walls and the curtains that hung around beds were not only beautiful but also provided insulation and added warmth. Floors, often made of handsome but cold stone, were covered with mats of woven rushes or Turkish carpets (which were also used as tablecloths and wall hangings). Sometimes bare floors were strewn with loose rushes and fragrant herbs.

One place that was always warm (much too warm at times) was the kitchen. A palace or great house might in fact have several kitchens, along with "kitchen offices" such as pantries and cellars. At Hampton Court, the kitchen complex had its own gatehouse, and the buildings were arranged around three courtyards. The offices included a spicery, where herbs and spices were kept; a chandlery, for the storage of candles and table linens; a confectionary, where desserts were prepared over the Elizabethan version of

Elizabeth, Countess of Shrewsbury—more famous as Bess of Hardwick Hall charcoal grills; a pastry house with four ovens; larders for the storage of meat, fish, and nuts and dried beans; a boiling house with a seventy-five-gallon copper pot for boiling meats and making soup stock; a pheasant yard; and cellars for wine and ale. Then there was the great kitchen itself, where meat could be turned on spits in six huge fireplaces. This kitchen had two serving hatches, at which servants picked up the prepared food to carry it on into the great hall. As many as two hundred people worked in the kitchens and offices; most of them also slept and ate their meals in the kitchen complex.

The kitchen of Windsor Castle in 1819; it would not have looked much different in Elizabeth's time.

Elizabeth and Her Court

The royal kitchens cooked a huge amount of food—of meats alone, for example, 8,200 sheep, 2,300 deer, 1,870 pigs, 1,240 oxen, 760 calves, and 53 wild boar in a single year. The queen fed hundreds of officials and courtiers in the great hall every day, around midday and again late in the afternoon. She herself usually preferred to dine quietly in her privy chamber, "not tied to hours of eating . . . , but following appetite," as she said; and she did not "delight in belly cheer," so ate only in moderate amounts. Her food was supplied by her own private kitchen. At Hampton Court this was located right under her "closet," or privy chamber, resulting in considerable irritation. Her lord treasurer explained that the combination of noises and smells from the kitchen "reboundeth up into the closet [so] that her highness cannot sit quiet nor without ill savor." Eventually she ordered her private kitchen relocated.

Another source of odor and annoyance arose from the sanitation facilities. Elizabeth's godson Sir John Harington once exclaimed in disgust, "Even in the goodliest and stateliest palaces of our realm, notwithstanding all our provisions of vaults, or sluices, or gates, or pains of poor folks in sweeping and scouring, yet still this same . . . saucy stink!" The queen used a closestool, an upholstered box with an opening in the top and a chamber pot inside. Some courtiers had their own closestools, but the rest of the court was supposed to use either the "house of easement," a large, multiseat outhouse, or the latrines at various locations throughout the palace. The situation was similar in the houses of the nobility. Toward the end of Elizabeth's reign, though, Harington came up with another alternative: the water closet. Elizabeth was quick to install this forerunner of the modern flush toilet in Richmond Palace.

The Earl of Leicester and Elizabeth enjoy playing lute and keyboard together while courtiers relax in the garden during the queen's visit to Kenilworth Castle.

THE QUEEN'S PROGRESS

With as many as 1500 people in residence at any given time, each royal palace could only be occupied for a month or two. At that point the latrines and other facilities would be filthy and the provisions from the surrounding area used up, so Elizabeth, her court, and the household would move on to another palace. Most summers, too, the queen went "on progress," visiting various nobles and other prominent subjects on their home estates. This gave her an opportunity to move among her people in the cities and countryside, as well as providing more time for the cleaning and resupplying of her palaces. Going on progress also saved her money, since those she visited were expected to feed, house, and entertain her and all the courtiers that traveled with her.

Elizabeth's most famous progress was that of 1575, which included her visit to Kenilworth Castle. The Earl of Leicester was her host there, and during her ten-day stay he did everything in his power to impress and delight her. She was greeted by poetic speeches, musicians, gentlemen and ladies dressed as characters from the legends of King Arthur, cannon salutes, and fireworks. After she came to her rooms, though, she remarked to Leicester that she had no view there of the castle's beautiful formal garden; during the night he had workmen lay out an identical garden beneath her windows. On the following days there were banquets, theatrical performances, dances, hunts, more fireworks, and even a country wedding.

Leicester had hired playwright George Gascoigne to compose all the entertainments; one of these was a water pageant. It featured two large models on the lake, one of a mermaid and the other of a dolphin—inside of which musicians and a singer were concealed. The most important festivity was planned for the last night: an elaborately costumed masque in which Juno, the ancient Roman goddess of marriage, would convince a virtuous maiden named "Zabeta" to marry. This was Leicester's way of suggesting that Elizabeth, too, should get married—and to him. Unfortunately, the masque was rained out. Elizabeth departed the next day as planned, hardly hearing the hastily written farewell poem that Gascoigne declaimed as he ran alongside her horse.

Councillors and Courtiers

The greatness which he affected was built upon true worth; esteeming fame more than riches, and noble actions far above nobility itself.

⁓FULKE GREVILLE, *THE LIFE OF THE RENOWNED SIR PHILIP SIDNEY*

ELIZABETH'S HOUSEHOLD INCLUDED MEN OF ALL RANKS and many functions. There were the numerous humble servants who worked in the kitchens, stables, and throughout the palace and grounds, and the upper servants who supervised them. There were household officials such as the steward and the chamberlain—the first responsible for the kitchen and its offices, the second for all matters to do with the royal lodgings. There were Serjeants-at-Arms, Yeomen of the Guard, and Gentlemen Pensioners to protect the queen. Looking after her private apartments were gentlemen and footmen of the privy chamber, grooms, and an Esquire of the Body, who saw that the presence chamber was guarded at night. For her entertainment, actors, jesters, and musicians could be summoned. And there were countless visitors and hangers-on, for the court was open to anyone who held the rank of gentleman or above.

Opposite: Sir Philip Sidney. Courtier, poet, diplomat, and warrior, he was considered a model gentleman and knight.

Among the notable men attending this diplomatic conference are Elizabeth's Lord Admiral Charles Howard (on the right, with his hand on the table). Elizabeth chose her councillors with care and required them to provide not only good advice but also "faithful hearts."

THE QUEEN'S ADVISERS

When Elizabeth came to the throne, England had fifty-seven peers—men who held the inherited title *duke, marquess, earl, viscount,* or *baron.* These were great lords, with large and wealthy estates. Most left those estates to visit or reside at court (bringing retinues of servants with them), attracted to the center of power. But Elizabeth did not surround herself only with noblemen. She also welcomed numerous gentlemen, men from nonnoble landholding families. During her reign she raised eighteen of these to the nobility as reward for their service to her and to England. (It is worth remembering, though, that this upper class of nobles and gentry made up only about 2 percent of England's population.)

The men who served the queen most diligently were the members of her Privy Council. The council had seventeen members, though not all of them regularly showed up for meetings. It met every day of the week, even Sunday, sometimes twice a day. The queen had chosen these advisers with such care that she rarely felt the need to attend their sessions. She had her own work to do, so she left them to theirs, but sent for councillors individually or in

Elizabeth and Her Court

small groups when she needed to confer with them. Sometimes she even summoned her most trusted councillors in the middle of the night, for she often worked very late.

The Privy Council supervised the officials who handled government affairs in the various regions of England as well as in Wales and Ireland. It enforced laws, regulated trade, and oversaw the military. It judged legal cases that affected the state or that could not be decided by other courts. It worked on foreign policy and national security. It kept an eye on plays and publications, making sure that nothing was performed or printed that might dangerously contradict the queen's policies or harm the national interest (freedom of the press was unknown in Europe at this time). It kept an eye on the mood of the country and on situations that could become problematic. Most of all, Elizabeth depended on her councillors to give her intelligent, informed advice on which she could base her decisions, and then to help her put those decisions into effect. She made this clear when she addressed them just a few days after she became queen:

> I shall require you all, my lords, to be assistant to me, that I with my ruling, and you with your service, may make a good account to Almighty God, and leave some comfort to our posterity on Earth.

> I mean to direct all mine actions by good advice and counsel. My meaning is to require of you all nothing more but faithful hearts, and of my good will you shall not doubt, using yourselves as good and loving subjects.

Indeed, most of these councillors served Elizabeth devotedly for the rest of their lives. There were three of them whom she relied on

William Cecil, Lord Burghley. He served Elizabeth devotedly from the day she became queen till the day he died, and there was no one she relied on more to help her govern her realm.

most of all. Sir William Cecil was so important to her that she nicknamed him her Spirit. "No prince in Europe ever had such a councillor as I have had in him," she said. He was a gentleman, but eventually she made him a baron, Lord Burghley. He first served as Principal Secretary, then became Lord Treasurer. The new Principal Secretary was Sir Francis Walsingham, a master of intelligence gathering and foreign diplomacy. The third member of this core group of advisers was one of Elizabeth's oldest and dearest friends—they'd known each other since they were eight—Robert Dudley, whom she made Earl of Leicester in 1564.

ROYAL FAVORITES

Before Leicester joined the Privy Council in 1562, he was Elizabeth's Master of Horse, responsible for the buying, training, and care of all the horses used by Elizabeth and her court. He was also expected to organize processions and a variety of entertainments, such as jousts, banquets, and plays. It was an ideal post for him, for he was an excellent and knowledgeable horseman with a love of pageantry and a talent for organization. Elizabeth was also enthusiastic about horses and entertainments, so Leicester spent time with the queen almost every day; they often went riding or hunting together in the afternoons. He seemed to be one of the few people with whom she could really relax and be herself. They were so close that for years there were rumors that she would marry him. But until his death in 1588 he remained, as she said, her "brother and best friend."

Elizabeth enjoyed being around men, especially handsome, witty, athletic men like Leicester. Not only did he ride superbly, but he also jousted and played tennis, and enjoyed fishing and archery. He dressed fashionably, sang well, and was a fine dancer. Like the queen, he read Greek and Latin and could converse fluently in Italian and French. He was able to discuss classical literature and current science, mathematics, and related fields. Other favorite courtiers possessed many of the same qualities and talents, together with a knack for pleasing the queen. She rewarded her favorites not only with her attention but also with gifts, knighthoods, offices in her household, and other opportunities to increase their wealth and importance.

Robert Dudley, Earl of Leicester, in the 1560s

The downside of being one of the queen's favorites was the risk of offending her. She was famous for her quick temper—the French ambassador commented, "When I see her enraged against any person whatever, I wish myself in Calcutta." Usually her anger died away almost as quickly as it had flared up. But if she felt that one of her favorites had seriously failed her or betrayed her in any way, she could be pitiless. When she found out that Sir Walter Raleigh had secretly married one of the young noblewomen in her service without her permission, Elizabeth had him imprisoned in the Tower of London for two months and then banished from court for five years. It was probably about this time that he wrote his poem "The Lie," which included the lines "Say to the court, it glows / And shines like rotten wood."

COURTLY POETS

Raleigh was one of a group of courtiers who were also talented poets. Elizabeth loved poetry, and so did many of those who surrounded her. Like the queen, some of them both wrote poems themselves and gave encouragement and rewards to other poets. Sometimes the courtier-poets addressed their poems directly to Elizabeth. They wrote praises of her beauty and wit or, when they were out of favor with her, lamented and complained about her coldness to them, as Robert Devereux, the Earl of Essex, did in these lines:

> I loved her whom all the world admired,
> I was refused of her that can love none;
> And my vain hopes, which far too high aspired,
> Is dead, and buried, and for ever gone.

Sir Philip Sidney, one of the finest poets of Elizabethan England, was widely regarded as the ideal courtier, perfect in manners and all the social graces. Like many of the queen's favorites, he was inspired by old tales of knightly deeds and yearned to fight for the queen in some glorious cause. Eventually he was sent with Leicester to the Low Countries (today's Netherlands and Belgium) to command English troops that were aiding the Protestant Dutch in their fight against Spanish rule. When Sidney died of a wound received in battle there, all England mourned. As his sister Mary wrote, his soul

A SONNET FROM SIDNEY

One of the most popular types of poetry in Elizabethan England was the sonnet, a fourteen-line poem with a fixed pattern of meter and rhyme. This form had been popularized by the fourteenth-century Italian poet Petrarch, whose works were imitated throughout western Europe. Sir Philip Sidney set the fashion for sonnet writing in England with his *Astrophil and Stella,* a sequence of 108 sonnets (plus eleven songs) that told a story of unrequited love. In sonnet 41, the lover describes how he won a joust—and not because of "sleight" (art), "use" (practice), luck, or even inherited talent.

Having this day my horse, my hand, my lance
   Guided so well that I obtained the prize,
   Both by the judgment of the English eyes
And of some sent from that sweet enemy France;
Horsemen my skill in horsemanship advance;
   Townfolks my strength; a daintier judge applies
   His praise to sleight, which from good use doth rise;
Some lucky wits impute it but to chance;
   Others, because of both sides I do take
My blood from them who did excel in this,
Think Nature me a man of arms did make.
How far they shoot awry! The true cause is,
   Stella looked on, and from her heavenly face
   Sent forth the beams which made so fair my race.

Edmund Spenser wrote most of his epic poem *The Faerie Queene* while he was serving in various government posts in Ireland.

was "brought to rest too soon" and his death deprived "the world of all / What man could show, which we perfection call." His poems, however, remained as "immortal monuments of [his] fair fame."

The greatest English poet of the time, most people agreed, was Edmund Spenser. Early in his career he had worked as Leicester's secretary and had become friends with Sidney. Raleigh was one of the first people to read Spenser's greatest work, *The Faerie Queene,* a romantic epic that celebrated Elizabeth, England, and the Protestant Church, with plenty of magical and knightly adventures mixed in. Raleigh's praise brought Spenser and his book to the queen's attention, and she rewarded Spenser with a generous annual pension for the rest of his life.

English literature flowered under Elizabeth, and there were many more poets and other writers working both at court and outside of it. There was one, though, who was the "soul of the age" in the words of fellow poet Ben Jonson, and that was William Shakespeare. Shakespeare was hardly a courtier, but he certainly had friends and admirers at court. He enjoyed the support of the Earl of Southampton and dedicated two long poems to him. Shakespeare's acting company, the Chamberlain's Men, was under the protection of Henry Carey, Lord Hunsdon, the queen's cousin. (All English acting companies during this period had a noble patron; for a time there was even a company of Queen's Men.)

Courtiers often went to the theaters just outside London's city

limits and saw Shakespeare's plays (and others) there, or sometimes they hosted private performances in their homes. The queen did not go to the theaters, but she loved plays, so the Chamberlain's Men were frequently invited to court to perform for her. For one of these occasions, Shakespeare apparently added a special epilogue to the play they performed:

A courtier entertains the queen and her ladies with witty conversation, or perhaps a poetry recitation, in this 1942 painting by English artist Frank Moss Bennett.

> As the dial hand tells o'er
> The same hours it had before, . . .
> So, most mighty Queen, we pray,
> Like the dial, day by day,
> You may lead the seasons on,
> Making new when old are gone.

Sir Francis Drake: explorer, privateer, and naval hero

ADVENTURE IN THE QUEEN'S NAME

During Elizabeth's reign, England became a major naval power, and many Englishmen sought wealth and adventure on the seas. Foremost among them was Sir Francis Drake, whom Elizabeth knighted in recognition of his achievement in sailing all the way around the world. His three-year voyage, from 1577 to 1580, opened up new sea routes to the English, increased the nation's prestige and confidence, and challenged Spain's naval dominance. It also earned handsome profits for all concerned—Drake, the expedition's investors, and the queen—thanks to successful raids on Spanish ships and settlements during its course. Drake went on to attack Spanish shipping on several other occasions, usually with Elizabeth's consent. She called him "our golden knight"—while the Spanish ambassador referred to him as "the master-thief of the unknown world."

Drake had received his training in seamanship under his cousin John Hawkins—a merchant-sailor in the eyes of the English, a pirate according to the Spanish and Portuguese. Hawkins was the first to import potatoes and tobacco from the New World to England. In the 1560s he was also one of the first Englishmen to participate in the slave trade, making three voyages in which he bought or captured slaves in Africa and then sold them in the West Indies. A more positive contribution to history was the range of improvements he made to the design of English ships, which became faster and more maneuverable as a result. Hawkins's improvements were successfully put to the test against the Spanish Armada in 1588. Thanks to the well-designed English ships and the bravery and resourcefulness of the men sailing them (along with help from the weather), the huge Spanish invasion force was driven off, putting an end to one of the greatest threats England ever faced.

The commanders of the English fleet included Drake and Hawkins, along with explorer Martin Frobisher. In the 1570s Frobisher had made three voyages to eastern Canada, hoping to find the Northwest Passage, a waterway to the Pacific Ocean. Another Elizabethan interested in exploration was Walter Raleigh, who named part of the New World "Virginia" after the Virgin Queen. Elizabeth refused to let Raleigh risk himself on a long voyage, but he organized exploratory and scientific expeditions to the Americas nevertheless. One of these even brought two Indian men back to visit England, where they were presented at court. Raleigh sponsored the first English colony in the New World, and although it failed, he continued to promote colonization of the Americas. His dream would not come true, though, till the founding of Jamestown under King James I.

English ships pursue the Spanish Armada over a churning sea.

Ladies of the Court

She did oft ask the ladies around her chamber if they loved to think of marriage,
and the wise ones did conceal well their liking hereto, as knowing
the Queen's judgement in this matter.
— SIR JOHN HARINGTON, *NUGAE ANTIQUAE*

ELIZABETH WAS A QUEEN IN A MAN'S WORLD. THE SCOTTISH preacher John Knox put the common opinion of female rulers most clearly and strongly: "To promote a Woman to bear rule, superiority, dominion, or empire above any Realm is repugnant to Nature; contrary to God, . . . it is the subversion of all good Order, of all equity and justice." Elizabeth could not agree with these sentiments (and she barred Knox from ever setting foot in England), but she was well aware that women in general were believed to be emotional, irrational, unreliable, and less intelligent than men. She knew that she was an exception to everything that was expected of women—but what made her exceptional was the fact that she was a queen. She had been divinely chosen, as the only surviving child of King Henry VIII, to rule her people: "I am God's creature, ordained to obey His appointment."

Opposite: Mary Rogers, wife of the queen's godson Sir John Harington. When her husband went to court, she generally stayed at home with their nine children. He called her "sweet Mall" and wrote her many letters in which he shared both the latest court gossip and his deepest feelings.

43

Henry Wriothesley, Earl of Southampton, had a secret romance with one of Elizabeth's Maids of Honor, Elizabeth Vernon, and then married her without the queen's permission. When the queen found out, she sent him to prison, but only for a short time.

Elizabeth's own extraordinary power did not spill over onto other women; except for the queen herself, government remained all male. Moreover, she discouraged her councillors and courtiers from bringing their wives to live with them at court. In part, probably, she was concerned about the expense of providing food and lodging for more people. She also preferred to be the sole focus of her courtiers' attention. For these reasons the number of women at court was small—probably thirty or fewer most of the time. Elizabeth did have female friends and companions, though, and the women of her household were of great importance to her daily comfort and well-being.

ATTENDING THE QUEEN

Throughout her childhood and youth, Elizabeth's closest companions were Katherine Ashley, her governess, and Blanche Parry, her former nurse. One of the first things she did when she became queen was reward them with important positions in her household—positions that would keep these faithful friends close. She made Parry Keeper of the Queen's Books. Ashley became Mistress of the Robes and First Lady of the Bedchamber. (Elizabeth also gave Ashley's husband a suitable office, Master of the Jewel House.)

As First Lady of the Bedchamber, one of Ashley's most important duties was to supervise the Maids of Honor. These were all girls from noble or gentle families, usually in their middle teens. Their parents competed fiercely to get these court positions for their daughters, whose service to the queen could boost their families' reputations. In addition, life at court gave Maids of Honor the chance to meet potential husbands, and parents hoped their daughters' marriages would make important connections among the noble and wealthy. Not surprisingly, these girls received much careful advice from their families, for instance:

> First, above all things not to forget to use daily prayers to Almighty God, then apply yourself wholly to the service of Her Majesty, with all meekness, love and obedience, wherein you must be diligent, secret [discreet] and faithful. . . . Use much silence, for that becometh maids, especially of your calling. Your speech and endeavors must ever tend to the good of all and to the hurt of none. If you have grace to follow these rules, you shall find the benefit.

Along with the Maids of Honor, the queen was served by Ladies of the Bedchamber. These were mainly married women, of all ages—from fifteen to eighty. Some spent their entire lives in the queen's service, utterly devoted to her. Elizabeth cared about them, too—even if she did sometimes lose her temper with them. Not only did she give them gifts of clothes and jewelry, but she comforted them when they suffered the death of a husband or child and sometimes even nursed them when they were ill.

The Maids and Ladies were not all on duty at the same time but had a rotating schedule. There were always six Maids of Honor and seven Ladies of the Bedchamber attending Elizabeth in the privy chamber and her bedroom. As many attendants as possible accompanied her whenever she appeared in public. In public or in private, she was never alone—even when she used her

Queen Elizabeth wrote the book of prayers that was decorated with this portrait of her by Nicholas Hilliard.

closestool, a lady stood by (and emptied the chamber pot afterward). And when Elizabeth went to bed at night, some of her ladies always slept in her room. As she said, "I do not live in a corner. A thousand eyes see all I do."

Because her ladies were always with her, Elizabeth expected them to be able to share her interests. They needed to be good horsewomen, talented in music and dancing, and, above all, intelligent. The queen loved learned books and tried to devote two or three hours every day to study. But when she didn't have time, or wanted more, she required her ladies to read to her as she dressed or performed other tasks. Many of the ladies enjoyed reading and learning for themselves, too; one writer commented on how they spent their leisure in "continual reading either of the Holy Scriptures or histories of our own or foreign nations about us, and . . . in writing volumes of their own, or translating of other men's into our English and Latin tongue."

The Maids of Honor and Ladies of the Bedchamber had both practical and ceremonial duties. They ran errands for the queen. They took care of her clothes and jewelry. They waited on her when she dined. When she made formal appearances, they strewed rose petals in her path and carried the train of her dress. Often the practical and the ceremonial combined. A German visitor to England in 1598 described a dinner at Greenwich Palace at which some of the queen's attendants played the following roles:

The Countess of Pembroke

Like her mother before her, Mary Sidney Herbert, Countess of Pembroke, was one of the queen's Ladies of the Bedchamber. Like her brother Sir Philip Sidney, she was a skilled poet and translator, as well as a patron of composers and poets. When Queen Elizabeth visited the Herbert country estate in the 1590s, Mary composed a poem to be performed in her honor. In it Elizabeth is called Astrea, after an immortal virgin who, according to Roman mythology, would bring a golden age of peace and justice to the earth. The speakers are two shepherds, Thenot and Piers; no matter what Thenot says, Piers scolds him for lying by not praising Astrea strongly enough. Here is an excerpt:

THENOT. ASTREA sees with Wisdom's sight,
　ASTREA works by Virtue's might,
　　And jointly both do stay in her.
PIERS. Nay take from them, her hand, her mind,
　The one is lame, the other blind
　　Shall still you lying stain her?

THENOT. Soon as ASTREA shows her face,
　Straight every ill avoids the place,
　　And every good aboundeth.
PIERS. Nay long before her face doth show,
　The last doth come, the first doth go,
　　How loud this lie resoundeth!

THENOT. ASTREA is our chiefest joy,
　Our chiefest guard against annoy,
　　Our chiefest wealth, our treasure.
PIERS. Where chiefest are, there others be,
　To us none else, but only she;
　　When wilt thou speak in measure?

Above: Mary Herbert, Countess of Pembroke

At last came an unmarried lady (we were told she was a Countess) and along with her a married one, bearing a tasting-knife. . . . When they had waited there a little while, the Yeomen of the Guard entered . . . , bringing in at each turn a course of twenty-four dishes . . . ; these dishes were received by a Gentleman in the same order they were brought, and placed upon the table, while the lady taster gave to each of the Guard a mouthful to eat of the particular dish he had brought, for fear of any poison. . . . At the end of all this ceremonial, a number of unmarried Ladies appeared, who with particular solemnity lifted the meat off the table and conveyed it into the Queen's inner and more private chamber, where, after she had chosen for herself, the rest goes to the Ladies of the Court.

THE DOMESTIC REALM

As Queen Elizabeth herself said, "There is a strong idea in the world that a woman cannot live unless she is married, or at all events that if she refrains from marriage she does so for some bad reason." Yet, even though the queen refused marriage, most other Englishwomen did expect to marry and have children. For women of the upper classes in particular, these were their most important duties.

An aristocratic woman also had to care for and run her household. There was much more to this than simply giving orders to servants. She had to make sure they did their work properly and efficiently, especially in the kitchen, the pantry, the dairy, and the laundry. She had special responsibilities toward her maidservants, whose welfare she was expected to watch over—so not only did she have to instruct them in their duties, but she had to keep them out of trouble, too. She might even arrange marriages for them and provide their dowries. Her responsibilities extended outside her own family and servants, to her neighbors and the tenants on her family's estates. She made sure that leftovers were distributed to the poor and medicines to the sick; she might even visit and nurse them herself. Her duty to provide charity also included giving hospitality to travelers.

A great family's estates supplied many or most of its needs—but anything that could not be grown or produced on the estates had to be purchased. This, too, was the lady's job. She had to figure out not only what was needed but exactly how much and whether the family budget would cover it—bearing in mind that between her family and servants, she might have a hundred or more people to provide for. And if her husband was away on business or in the queen's service, she might have to see to the running of the estates themselves. Women other than the queen might not have any political power, but they were in some ways queens of their own domestic realms.

Chrysogona Baker, the daughter of a gentleman knighted by Queen Elizabeth. When Chrysogona was seventeen she married a lord and became mistress of a great household.

5

Noble Children

Boy Jack, I have made a clerk write fair my poor words for thine use. . . .
Ponder them in thy hours of leisure, and play with them till
they enter thy understanding.

⟞LETTER FROM ELIZABETH TO HER FIFTEEN-YEAR-OLD GODSON

THERE WERE FEW CHILDREN AT ELIZABETH'S COURT—
mainly just some pageboys and the boys who sang in her chapel
choir. Many of her advisers and courtiers, however, did have children at home, although they might not see much of them. Noble
families were often separated when parents, especially fathers, were
required at court or on the queen's business elsewhere. But this did
not keep parents from loving and caring about their children. For
example, Sir Henry Sidney, who was an official in Elizabeth's government in Wales and Ireland, wrote a letter to his son Robert in
which he said, "I love thee, boy, well. . . . God bless you, my sweet
child, in this world forever, as I in this world find myself happy in
my children." Lord Burghley was another devoted father, as related
by a gentleman who served in his household: "If he could get his
table set round with his little children he was then in his kingdom."

Opposite: A mother holds her baby on the day of its baptism. The baby grasps a piece of coral, which wealthy families often gave their children to teethe on.

51

Children may have been cherished all the more because so many babies died during or soon after birth—135 out of every 1,000, according to one estimate—making those who lived seem precious indeed. But the surviving babies were not out of danger. Sanitation and medical knowledge were both limited in Elizabethan England, and the young were especially vulnerable to disease. Numerous children died at a young age, even among the most prosperous families. Anne Cecil de Vere, Countess of Oxford, lost both her children. After her two-day-old son died, she wrote a series of poems that expressed the terrible grief of parents in such a situation:

> The heavens, death, and life have conjured my ill:
> For death hath take away the breath of my son:
> The heavens receive, and consent, that he hath done:
> And my life doth keep me here against my will.

If the countess's children had lived, they would no doubt have been brought up like others of their class. No matter how loving parents were, wealthy families employed nursemaids and other servants to do most of the child care. Even breast-feeding was usually done by a servant, for about two years. After that, the wet nurse might remain in the household as a caretaker and close friend, especially if her charge was a girl.

Children spent their first months tightly wrapped in swaddling bands, since people believed that babies needed to be immobilized in order for their spines and limbs to grow straight. After that, boys and girls alike were dressed in long gowns. At six or seven, with ceremony and celebration, a boy was breeched—that is, given his first pair of breeches, or pants. From then on he dressed like an adult man. Girls might be very young when they started wearing miniature versions of adult clothing, including stiff, corsetlike bodices. This could have unhealthy results, which one father discovered when he had a doctor examine his two-year-old daughter: "His judgment was that her bodice was her pain and hindered her lungs to grow, and truth the surgeon found her breast bone pressed very deeply inwards and he said two of her ribs were broken."

Childhood was not all discomfort, of course. Noble boys and girls had plenty of toys to play with, including dolls and tops and (for boys) toy swords. They had board games, including chess and checkers. They also played the sixteenth-century versions of such games as hide-and-seek, blind man's buff, leapfrog, and red rover.

EDUCATION

Parents gave children their earliest lessons in manners and religion. Between the ages of three and five, noble children began to receive instruction from one or more private tutors. Boys and girls alike learned reading and writing (which were taught as separate subjects) and basic math.

Around the age of seven, education became more serious. Children of both sexes might continue to be tutored, with languages, philosophy, and other subjects added to the basics. Some boys were sent to another noble family to serve the master of the house as a page and learn adult skills from him. Girls, too, might for

Boys wore long gowns until they reached the age of six or seven.

a time go to live with another family, where the mistress of the house would oversee their education. Boys had the additional option of attending grammar school, where the main subject was Latin, the language of learning throughout Europe at this time. Generally they also learned Greek and perhaps Hebrew, as well as logic, the art of public speaking, and some sciences.

Although girls could not attend grammar school, many received excellent educations from their tutors. Elizabeth herself was one of the best educated women in England. When she was a girl, her step-mother Catherine Parr decided that she should be taught as well as any prince in Europe. One of her tutors was the great scholar Roger Ascham, who found the young Elizabeth to be an admirable student. "Her memory long keeps what it quickly picks up," he said at one time. After she became queen, she continued to study with him, and he bragged that "besides her perfect readiness in Latin, Italian, French and Spanish, she readeth here now at Windsor more Greek every day" than some learned men "doth read Latin in a whole week."

Ascham's educational techniques came to be admired so much that Burghley and some other gentlemen at court persuaded him to write a book, *The Schoolmaster.* In it Ascham condemned the common practice of beating reluctant students, arguing that "children were sooner allured by Love, than driven by Beating, to attain good Learning." He laid out a program, based on the Bible and the Greek and Latin classics, to foster "truth of Religion, Honesty in living, right Order in Learning." He also recommended rounding out a boy's education with physical and social skills:

To ride comely, to run fair at the tilt or ring, to play at all weapons, to shoot fair in bow, or surely in gun, to vault lustily; to run, to leap, to wrestle, to swim; to dance comely, to sing and play of instruments cunningly; to hawk, to hunt, to play at tennis and all pastimes generally, which be joined with labour, used in open place and in the daylight, containing either some fit exercise for war, or some pleasant pastime for peace, be not only comely and decent, but also very necessary for a courtly gentleman to use.

Similarly, noble girls usually learned to dance, sing, and play at least one musical instrument. Sometimes they were also taught how to make medicines and cordials, and perhaps perfumes. These were all skills found among the ladies of Elizabeth's court, and they could be useful and enjoyable for a noblewoman in her own home as well. The ability to do fine embroidery, too, was much cultivated. Upper-class girls and women embroidered their clothes, their gloves, their handkerchiefs, their purses, their gifts to others, the cushions and draperies in their homes—almost anything made of cloth. They also did spinning and sewing for their families, just as women of other classes did.

BECOMING AN ADULT

Many upper-class boys went on to higher education, starting as young as fifteen. They might attend one of England's two universities, Oxford and Cambridge, or study at the Inns of Court in London. At the universities they studied most of the same subjects as in grammar school, but more extensively. At the Inns they learned their country's laws and the procedures of Parliament. Aristocratic young men often rounded off their education with a long tour of continental Europe, especially Italy.

The all-important step into full adulthood was marriage. Among the upper classes, weddings were arranged by the parents largely for the purpose of making connections with other important or wealthy

LORD BURGHLEY
SENDS HIS DAUGHTER A GIFT

Anne Cecil had recently turned eleven years old when her father, Lord Burghley, wrote her this poem to accompany his New Year's present to her:

As years do grow, so cares increase;
    And time will move to look to thrift:*
Though years in me work nothing less,
    Yet, for your years, and New Year's gift,
    This housewife's toy is now my shift!
      To set you on work, some thrift to feel,
    I send you now a Spinning Wheel.

But one thing first, I wish and pray,
    Lest thirst of thrift might soon you tire,
Only to spin one pound a day,
    And play the rest, as time require:
    Sweat not! (oh fie!) fling rock in fire!
      God send, who send'th all thrift and wealth,
    You, long years; and your father, health!

*This poem plays with the various meanings of *thrift*, which could refer to careful management of time and money, success through hard work, prosperity, and healthy, vigorous growth.

Above: Baron Cobham, one of the realm's most influential noblemen, with his wife, Frances (*right*), and members of their family. One of the little girls, Elizabeth, would grow up to wed Lord Burghley's son, Robert Cecil.

families—love was often not a factor. Although the church, and people in general, frowned on parents compelling a child to marry someone she or he disliked, it did happen. The playwright Thomas Heywood described this situation and how unhappily it could turn out: "How often have forced contracts been made to add land to land, not love to love? And to unite houses to houses, not hearts to hearts? which hath been the occasion that men have turned monsters, and women devils." Girls, who were raised to be unquestioningly obedient, were most likely to be pressured into marriages they didn't want. Among the nobility, they usually married in their teens, while men typically waited until their twenties.

At the same time, Elizabethan songs and poetry celebrated love and romance. Young people at court probably couldn't help being influenced by poetic notions of ideal love, and there was much flirting between male courtiers and the Maids of Honor. Some relationships, though, went beyond flirting. Secret romances occurred from time to time, often with hard consequences, including disgrace, banishment from the court, and even imprisonment.

The queen was very protective of her Maids of Honor, whose families had trusted them to her guardianship. She was almost as eager to arrange suitable marriages for them as their own parents were and did not like to see them ruining their chances or being taken advantage of by inappropriate suitors. She would use all her powers of persuasion to discourage unpromising matches—but she also did not hesitate to encourage unions that she thought would be beneficial to both bride and groom. No matter what, though, it was important to her to be in control of everything around her—including the private lives of her ladies and courtiers.

Celebrations and Spectacles

After supper there were two delights presented unto Her Majesty:
curious fireworks, and a sumptuous banquet. . . .
— WILLIAM LYLY, 1591

FAMILY EVENTS, SUCH AS WEDDINGS AND CHRISTENINGS, gave the upper classes many opportunities to host and attend grand festivities. In spite of her personal feelings about marriage, Elizabeth enjoyed weddings. Sometimes she even allowed noble weddings to be celebrated at court. Wherever an aristocratic wedding was held, days of feasting, music, and dancing—often with the addition of theatrical performances—made these occasions to remember.

Holidays, too, brought people together in celebration. Male courtiers, however, were expected to remain at court during Christmas, so their families often observed the holiday without them. But the season at court was splendid. The queen liked to observe Christmas itself as a day of prayer, but then the twelve days after Christmas were given over to banquets, dancing, games, and merriment. Queen and courtiers exchanged gifts on New Year's Day

Opposite: Dancing was a favorite pastime at Elizabeth's court. She loved to dance and to watch her ladies and courtiers dancing, too.

59

Elizabeth in her coronation robes and crown, holding the orb and scepter that symbolized her authority

or Twelfth Night (January 6). Elizabeth especially enjoyed seeing plays at this season, and some years as many as eleven productions were presented at court during Christmastime.

ROYAL OCCASIONS

From the very beginning of her reign, Elizabeth had an appreciation and flair for the dramatic. Her coronation was in many ways a theatrical spectacle. She was determined to put on a show of magnificence to impress both her people and the foreign ambassadors and agents in England, so that no one would have any doubts about her and her nation's strength. Moreover, she wanted to show her love for the people and to establish a lasting bond with them. She succeeded.

The day before the actual coronation, there was a four-mile procession through the streets of London. Elizabeth's fur-trimmed gown was made of cloth of gold and silver—twenty-three yards of fabric in all. She rode in a mule-drawn litter upholstered in white satin, with her Gentlemen Pensioners walking alongside. Also accompanying her were scarlet-clad trumpeters, footmen with roses (the symbol of Elizabeth's family) embroidered on their clothing, the members of her Privy Council in rich satin robes, thirty-nine ladies wearing crimson velvet gowns, gorgeously dressed courtiers—in all about two thousand people. The day was gray, with some snow flurries, but Elizabeth's retinue "so sparkled with jewels and gold collars that they cleared the air," according to an ambassador from Venice.

In spite of the weather, the processional route was lined with

Elizabeth and Her Court

cheering crowds of Londoners eager to see their new queen. People approached her frequently to give her sprigs of rosemary and other little gifts. She always stopped to speak with them, and she was equally attentive to those who could not reach her: "Her grace, by holding up her hands and merry countenance to such as stood far off, and most tender and gentle language to those that stood nigh to her grace, did declare herself no less thankfully to receive her people's goodwill than they lovingly offered it to her." She also stopped along the route to greet the Lord Mayor and other London city officials, to watch pageants, to hear speeches made by students, and to listen to children read poems in her honor.

The next day's activities began with Elizabeth's procession to Westminster Abbey; she walked on a blue carpet, and two noble-men held a canopy over her head while a duchess carried the train of her coronation robes. At Westminster, hundreds of candles and torches lit the beautiful medieval church, where most of the English nobility had gathered. At the end of a solemn worship service accompanied by magnificent music, Elizabeth took her coronation oath. Then she stood upon a platform in front of the altar, and the people were asked if they accepted her as their queen. They roared their approval, echoed by such a noise of "organs, fifes, trumpets, and drums playing, the bells also ringing, it seemed as if the world were come to an end," reported the Venetian ambassador. Then at last Elizabeth sat in her throne, received the coronation ring that symbolized her union with her people, and the crown was placed on her head.

The coronation was followed by banquets, jousts, and revels lasting for days. By the end of the 1570s, many of these festivities were being reenacted every year. In London and other places in England, November 17 came to be celebrated as Accession Day, the anniversary of Elizabeth's coming to the throne. Accession Day had a serious aspect, as the English people listened to sermons and prayed for the well-being of their queen and nation. But this was also an occasion for "joyful ringing of bells, running at tilt, and festival mirth, in testimony to their affectionate love towards her."

"WE ARE FROLIC"

Courtiers enjoyed a good amount of leisure time, which they might spend riding and hunting, at archery, playing tennis or lawn bowling, or strolling outdoors in the gardens or indoors in the galleries. Indoor pastimes included playing cards, chess, or backgammon; reading or listening to someone else read aloud; and simply enjoying good conversation with friends. And it seems that a great many courtiers, as well as the queen, were passionately fond of music.

In Elizabethan England, there were no radios, CD players, or iPods. If you wanted music, you either had to make it yourself or have musical friends or employees. Elizabeth did both. She played the lute and a small keyboard called a virginal, and her household included nearly a hundred singers and musicians, some from Italy and the Low Countries. A number of her ladies and courtiers sang and played music, and many nobles also employed their own household musicians. People entertained themselves with madrigals, songs for a small number of unaccompanied singers, each singing a different melody; airs, songs for one singer and instrumental accompaniment; pieces for solo lute or keyboard; and pieces for groups of recorders, lutes, or viols (early members of the violin family) of different sizes.

The Elizabethans also expected music to be part of many of their other activities, from processions and jousts to plays to

Children in a noble family play chess and cards as their parents and grandmother look on.

church services. The music for services in Elizabeth's chapel was especially glorious. The organist was William Byrd, one of Europe's greatest keyboard and choral composers. The choir of twelve boys and thirty-two men was praised by all who heard them; a Danish ambassador said that a service he attended in the royal chapel was "so melodiously sung . . . as a man half dead might thereby have been quickened."

Music naturally went hand in hand with dancing, another favorite activity of Elizabeth and her courtiers and part of almost any celebration. "We are frolic here in Court: such dancing in the Privy Chamber of country dances before the Queen's Majesty, who is exceedingly pleased therewith," wrote the Earl of Worcester in September 1602, adding, "Irish tunes are at this time most pleasing." One country dance, originally from France, was the

SUNDAY AT GREENWICH PALACE

Pageantry was a way of life for Elizabeth, and she made the most of any opportunity she had to appear before her people. Even her walk to the royal chapel every Sunday was a spectacle, one that German traveler Paul Hentzner was privileged to witness in 1598:

We were admitted . . . into the Presence Chamber . . . through which the Queen commonly passes in her way to Chapel. At the door stood a Gentleman dressed in velvet, with a gold chain, whose office was to introduce to the Queen any person of distinction that came to wait on her. It was Sunday, when there is usually the greatest attendance of nobility. . . . [All] waited the Queen's coming out; which she did from her own apartment, when it was time to go to prayers, attended in the following manner.

First went Gentlemen, Barons, Earls, Knights of the Garter, all richly dressed and bare-headed; next came the Chancellor . . . between two [men], one of which carried the Royal Sceptre, the other the Sword of State in a red scabbard. . . . Next came the Queen, in the sixty-fifth year of her age, as we were told, very majestic. . . . That day she was dressed in white silk, bordered with pearls the size of beans, and over it a mantle of black silk, shot with silver threads. . . .

Queen Elizabeth in the late 1570s

As she went along in all this state and magnificence, she spoke very graciously, first to one, then to another, whether foreign ministers, or those who attended for different reasons, in English, French and Italian. . . . Whoever speaks to her, it is kneeling; now and then she raises some with her hand. . . . Wherever she turned her face, as she was going along, everybody fell down on their knees.

The Ladies of the Court followed next to her, very handsome and well-shaped, and for the most part dressed in white; she was guarded on each side by the Gentlemen Pensioners, fifty in number, with gilt battle-axes. In the antechapel next the hall where we were, petitions were presented to her, and she received them most graciously, which occasioned the acclamation of "Long live Queen Elizabeth!" She answered it with, "I thank you, my good people."

brawl; it went, as poet Sir John Davies described, "Upward and downward, forth and back again, / To this side and to that, and turning round." Courtly dances included the stately pavane and the lively galliard, which the queen was especially fond of. At one time, as a courtier observed, "six or seven galliards of a morning, besides music and singing, were her ordinary exercise." In her later years, Elizabeth no longer danced much, but she always watched the court dances with both enjoyment and a critical eye. A French ambassador noted, "When her maids dance, she follows the cadence with her head, hand and foot. She rebukes them if they do not dance to her liking, and without doubt she is mistress of the art."

Palace Problems

Uneasy lies the head that wears a crown.
— William Shakespeare, *Henry IV, Part 2*

THE REIGN OF ELIZABETH I WAS A GOLDEN AGE FOR ENGLAND, but it was not a perfect one. As in all other times and places, there were hardships and difficulties. We have seen some of them already, from annoyances such as smelly outhouses to tragedies such as the deaths of young children. The queen and her courtiers, in spite of all their privileges, could not avoid encountering troubles. And many troubles came to them precisely because of their lofty position in government and society.

HEALTH HAZARDS

Diseases such as bubonic plague and smallpox afflicted people of all classes. Even the queen was not safe—she nearly died of smallpox in 1562. Some of her courtiers did die of the disease, and others came close to it. One of those who suffered worst was Lady Mary

Opposite: Elizabeth's cousin Mary Queen of Scots lost her throne and fled to England, where she lived under house arrest for many years. There she became the focus of numerous treasonous plots against Elizabeth until, finally, the English monarch was forced to order her execution.

Sidney. As one of Elizabeth's most devoted Ladies of the Bedchamber, she stayed by the queen's side and nursed her through her illness. But in doing so, she caught smallpox herself. The disease left her so badly scarred that her husband, who had been in Wales at the time, wrote, "I left her a full, fair lady, in mine eyes at least the fairest, and when I returned, I found her as foul a lady as the smallpox could make her. . . . Now she lives solitary." Lady Mary left court and rarely returned; when she did, she would not leave her chamber. But Elizabeth never forgot her friend's faithful kindness and visited her privately, both at court and at the Sidney home.

Other serious diseases common during this period were dysentery, measles, malaria, and influenza; the last two were both, rather confusingly, sometimes called "the ague," referring to the symptoms of fever and chills. Such illnesses could afflict both rich and poor equally. Others were more common among the well-to-do, particularly conditions related to overeating. For example, wealthy Elizabethans tended to eat a lot of meat, and this extremely high-protein diet could contribute to kidney stones and gout (a painful swelling of the feet and legs).

The English upper classes often indulged a love of sweets. Many ladies of Elizabeth's court and of noble houses enjoyed making preserves and candies, which their friends and families no doubt enjoyed eating. Elizabeth herself loved cakes, tarts, and fritters. As a result she suffered from serious tooth decay; a German visitor who saw her when she was in her sixties reported that her teeth were black— "a defect the English seem subject to, from their too great use of sugar." In her old age her teeth gave her so much pain that she could only eat soups, stews, and soft foods. Many of those around her no doubt suffered from dental disease just as bad or worse.

PLOTS AND INTRIGUES

As Edmund Spenser had a character in one of his poems comment, the court could be a place

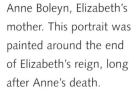

> Where each one seeks with malice and with strife,
> To thrust downe other into foule disgrace,
> Himselfe to raise.

Courtiers competed with one another for high positions and the queen's favor, and many were not above scheming against a rival. The court was a hotbed of gossip, too; it was easy to spread a rumor to discredit an enemy. Some courtiers greatly resented the queen's devotion to her favorites and looked for ways to undermine them. Problems also arose when favorites tried to take advantage of the queen. And her temper could be unpredictable—over the years, she gave many a courtier and lady a tongue-lashing. Usually, however, the objects of her anger were soon back in her good graces, unless they had committed a truly serious offense.

Anne Boleyn, Elizabeth's mother. This portrait was painted around the end of Elizabeth's reign, long after Anne's death.

The worst of all offenses was treason. During the course of Elizabeth's reign, there were several conspiracies to overthrow or assassinate her. Most of these plots centered on her cousin, Mary Queen of Scots. Some people thought that Mary had a stronger claim to the English throne than Elizabeth because, they believed, the marriage of Elizabeth's mother to King Henry VIII had not been legitimate. In addition, Mary was a Catholic. The Catholic powers, especially Spain, were determined to win England back to their church, one way or another. Spanish agents plotted with English Catholics to invade England and place Mary on the throne.

The threats against her sometimes depressed Elizabeth; at one point she expressed her feelings in a poem:

The doubt of future foes exiles my present joy,

And wit me warns to shun such snares as threaten mine annoy.

For falsehood now doth flow, and subjects' faith doth ebb,

Which would not be, if reason ruled or wisdom weaved the web.

On the other hand, she was heartened when she discovered that tens of thousands of her subjects had signed a document known as the Bond of Association. It was 1584, and Sir Francis Walsingham had uncovered yet another assassination plot designed to make Mary queen. The signers of the Bond all swore that if Elizabeth were killed, they would personally hunt down both the murderer and "any that have, may, or shall pretend title to come to this crown by the untimely death of her Majesty so wickedly procured." When Elizabeth next spoke to Parliament, she told them:

> I am not unmindful of your Oath made in the Association man-
> ifesting your great goodwills and affections . . . done (I protest to
> God) before I heard of it or ever thought of such a matter. . . .
> Which I do acknowledge as a perfect argument of your true
> hearts and great zeal for my safety, so shall my bond be stronger
> tied to greater care for your good.

WAR

The situation with Mary Queen of Scots grew worse and worse. She had been living under house arrest for many years, and for a long time Elizabeth tried to maintain friendly relations with her. She had always given her the benefit of the doubt, partly because Mary was one of her closest living relatives and partly because Elizabeth believed that monarchs ruled by divine right and so their lives were sacred. If Mary, a monarch, could be condemned to death, so could Elizabeth. But at last it was proven that Mary was directly involved in a conspiracy against Elizabeth. In 1587, with great regret, Elizabeth signed the order to have Mary executed for treason.

After years of hostilities between the two nations, this was the excuse Spain needed to declare all-out war against England. The Spanish king, Philip II, had already been building his naval forces; now he stepped up his preparations for invasion. The queen authorized Sir Francis Drake to make a preemptive strike. He attacked the harbor of Cádiz, where he burned naval stores and thirty-seven Spanish ships, then headed out to sea, where he captured dozens more. His actions "singed the King of Spain's beard," he bragged—but he, and everyone else, knew he had only delayed the inevitable. "I assure your honor," Drake wrote to Sir Francis Walsingham, "the like preparation was never heard of nor known, as the King of Spain hath and daily maketh to invade England. . . . Prepare in England strongly, and most by sea. Stop him now, and stop him ever. Look well to the coasts."

Through the first half of 1588, Elizabeth tried to negotiate a peace with Spain. By the time she gave up, the Spanish Armada had set sail. The fleet of 130 ships carried thirty thousand men—along with thousands of copies of a proclamation from the pope, head of the Catholic Church, blessing the invasion and exhorting the English to rebel against Elizabeth. When the people of England found out about this proclamation, they were more determined than ever to repel the Spanish. All along the southern coast, they readied their defenses, and the English fleet set sail.

Led by Lord Admiral Charles Howard and Sir Francis Drake, Elizabeth's ships met the Armada on July 21, beginning a week of sea battles in the English Channel. By the twenty-ninth the English had the upper hand and the Spanish were on the run. The weather did the rest, with storms blowing the enemy ships off course and destroying many on the rocky coasts of Scotland and Ireland. Spain lost forty-four ships and around 19,000 men; England lost no ships and only a hundred men in the fighting (although by the end of the campaign thousands of sailors were dying of typhus and scurvy).

After it was all over, the English stayed braced for trouble, for across the Channel, in the Low Countries, a Spanish army was being assembled, ready to take ship for England at any moment. But with no naval support for his army, King Philip at last gave up his invasion plans. By the end of August, Elizabeth and her people were celebrating their victory.

It was perhaps the most glorious time in a glorious age. There was no one now who could doubt the might of England and the ability of its queen. Even Pope Sixtus V, who had encouraged King Philip to invade, had to admit to a certain admiration of Elizabeth: "Just look how well she governs! She is only a woman, only mistress of half an island, and yet she makes herself feared by Spain, by France, . . . by all."

The rest of Elizabeth's reign was not without its troubles, and Spain eventually began once more to plot the conquest of England. It never succeeded. Elizabeth kept war from coming to England's shores, and kept the peace among her people at home. She was no more perfect than any other ruler—or human being—but she embodied a greatness that has inspired women and men ever since. Her cousin and successor, James I, expressed it well in the epitaph he ordered inscribed on her tomb:

> The mother of this her country, the nurse of religion and learning; for perfect skill of very many languages, for glorious endowments, as well of mind as of body, a prince incomparable.

Elizabeth would have liked that.

GLOSSARY

Catholic refers to the branch of Christianity under the authority of the pope

cordial an alcoholic drink flavored with fruit, herbs, spices, or nuts, originally meant to be taken as medicine

courtier a person who lived at or regularly attended a ruler's court

dowry money, property, and goods supplied by a bride's family for her to bring into her marriage

gentry gentlemen and their families; nonnoble landowners who lived off the income of their estates

joust a contest in which two riders armed with lances rode at each other and tried to knock each other from their horses

masque a relatively short play combining poetry, songs, and dances. The characters were usually symbolic or mythological figures. Court masques were performed by courtiers rather than professional actors.

militia a locally based armed force made up of regular citizens (as opposed to professional soldiers). In Elizabethan England, all able-bodied males sixteen to sixty might be required to serve in the militias in a national emergency.

patron someone who gives financial support or other assistance and encouragement to an artist, musician, writer, etc.

Protestant refers to Christians who reject the authority of the pope and many practices and beliefs of the Catholic Church

scurvy a disease resulting from lack of vitamin C in the diet

tilt joust; a tournament of jousts

typhus a bacterial infection, usually transmitted by lice, that was common in crowded conditions such as those aboard ship

FOR FURTHER READING

Adams, Simon. *Elizabeth I: The Outcast Who Became England's Queen*. Washington, DC: National Geographic, 2005.

Ashby, Ruth. *Elizabethan England*. New York: Benchmark Books, 1999.

Crompton, Samuel Willard. *Queen Elizabeth and England's Golden Age*. Philadelphia: Chelsea House, 2005.

Greenblatt, Miriam. *Elizabeth I and Tudor England*. New York: Benchmark Books, 2002.

Hilliam, Paul. *Elizabeth I: Queen of England's Golden Age*. New York: Rosen Publishing Group, 2004.

Hinds, Kathryn. *Life in the Renaissance: The Court*. New York: Benchmark Books, 2004.

Lace, William W. *Defeat of the Spanish Armada*. San Diego: Lucent Books, 1997.

Lace, William W. *Elizabeth I and Her Court*. San Diego: Lucent Books, 2002.

Lace, William W. *Elizabethan England*. San Diego: Lucent Books, 2005.

Olson, Steven P. *Sir Walter Raleigh: Explorer for the Court of Queen Elizabeth*. New York: Rosen Publishing Group, 2003.

Paige, Joy. *Sir Francis Drake: Circumnavigator of the Globe and Privateer for Queen Elizabeth*. New York: Rosen Publishing Group, 2003.

Weatherly, Myra. *Elizabeth I: Queen of Tudor England*. Minneapolis: Compass Point Books, 2005.

ONLINE INFORMATION

Best, Michael. *Shakespeare's Life and Times*.
   http://ise.uvic.ca/Library/SLT/intro/introsubj.html

Encyclopedia Britannica. *Guide to Shakespeare*.
   http://www.britannica.com/shakespeare

Historic Royal Palaces. *Hampton Court Palace: History*.
   http://hrp.org.uk/hampton/history

Jokinen, Anniina. *16th Century Renaissance English Literature (1485–1603)*.
   http://www.luminarium.org/renlit

The Norton Anthology of English Literature.
   http://www.wwnorton.com/nael/16century/welcome.htm

Renaissance: The Elizabethan World.
   http//:elizabethan.org

Shakespeare Resource Center.
   http://www.bardweb.net

Thomas, Heather. *Queen Elizabeth I (1533–1603)*.
   http://www.elizabethi.org/us/

Elizabeth and Her Court

SELECTED BIBLIOGRAPHY

Ault, Norman, ed. *Elizabethan Lyrics from the Original Texts.* 3rd ed. New York: William Sloane Associates, 1949.

Budiansky, Stephen. *Her Majesty's Spymaster: Elizabeth I, Sir Francis Walsingham, and the Birth of Modern Espionage.* New York: Viking, 2005.

Clarke, Amanda. *Growing Up in Elizabethan Times.* London: B. T. Batsford, 1980.

Dunn, Jane. *Elizabeth and Mary: Cousins, Rivals, Queens.* New York: Knopf, 2004.

Editors of Time-Life Books. *What Life Was Like in the Realm of Elizabeth: England AD 1533–1603.* Alexandria, VA: Time-Life Books, 1998.

Haydn, Hiram, ed. *The Portable Elizabethan Reader: The Portrait of a Golden Age.* New York: Viking, 1960.

Logan, George M., et al., eds. *The Norton Anthology of English Literature.* Vol. 1B, *The Sixteenth Century, The Early Seventeenth Century.* 7th ed. New York: W. W. Norton, 2000.

Orlin, Lena Cowen. *Elizabethan Households: An Anthology.* Washington, DC: The Folger Shakespeare Library, 1995.

Plowden, Alison. *Tudor Women: Queens and Commoners.* New York: Atheneum, 1979.

Pritchard, R. E., ed. *Shakespeare's England: Life in Elizabethan and Jacobean Times.* Stroud, Gloucestershire: Sutton Publishing, 1999.

Rowse, A. L. *The Elizabethan Renaissance: The Cultural Achievement.* New York: Charles Scribner's Sons, 1972.

Rowse, A. L. *The England of Elizabeth: The Structure of Society.* Madison: University of Wisconsin Press, 1978.

Shapiro, James. *A Year in the Life of William Shakespeare: 1599.* New York: HarperCollins, 2005.

Singman, Jeffrey L. *Daily Life in Elizabethan England.* Westport, CT: Greenwood Press, 1995.

Thurley, Simon. *The Royal Palaces of Tudor England: Architecture and Court Life 1460–1547.* New Haven: Yale University Press, 1993.

Weir, Alison. *The Life of Elizabeth I.* New York: Ballantine Books, 1998.

SOURCES FOR QUOTATIONS

This series of books tries to bring the people of Elizabethan England to life by quoting their own words whenever possible. When necessary for clarity, however, we have modernized the Elizabethan spellings preserved in the sources. All Shakespeare quotes are from William Shakespeare, *Complete Works, Compact Edition,* edited by Stanley Wells et al. (Oxford: Clarendon Press, 1988).

Chapter 1

p. 9 "I am already bound": Dunn, *Elizabeth and Mary,* p. 122.

p. 11 "I know I have" and "Let tyrants" and "my faithful": Logan, *The Norton Anthology of English Literature,* p. 597.

p. 12 "I will have here": Plowden, *Tudor Women,* p. 158.

p. 12 "O Goddesse": Logan, *The Norton Anthology of English Literature,* pp. 628–629.

p. 12 "We did nothing": Plowden, *Tudor Women,* p. 162.

p. 12 "If ever any person": ibid., p. 155.

p. 13 "There was never": Weir, *The Life of Elizabeth I,* p. 221.

p. 15 "This other Eden": Shakespeare, *Richard II,* act 2, scene 1.

p. 17 "descended by father": Dunn, *Elizabeth and Mary,* p. 8.

p. 17 "it is not she": Budiansky, *Her Majesty's Spymaster,* p. 49.

p. 17 "Queen Elizabeth would set": Weir, *The Life of Elizabeth I,* p. 220.

Chapter 2

p. 19 "Many of the splendid": Weir, *The Life of Elizabeth I,* p. 244.

p. 19 "The ancient manors": Orlin, *Elizabethan Households,* pp. 9–10.

p. 21 "ingeniously composed": Weir, *The Life of Elizabeth I,* p. 242.

p. 21 "the water pours": Shapiro, *A Year in the Life of William Shakespeare,* p. 26.

p. 22 "a warm nest": Editors of Time-Life, *What Life Was Like in the Realm of Elizabeth,* p. 36.

p. 23 "Search Windsor Castle": Shakespeare, *The Merry Wives of Windsor,* act 5, scene 5.

p. 24 "more glass": Editors of Time-Life, *What Life Was Like in the Realm of Elizabeth,* p. 50.

p. 24 "each arbor": Logan, *The Norton Anthology of English Literature,* p. 1288.

p. 25 "Where being seated": ibid., p. 1289.

p. 27 "not tied" and "delight in": Weir, *The Life of Elizabeth I,* p. 252.

p. 27 "reboundeth up": Thurley, *The Royal Palaces of Tudor England,* p. 161 (spelling modernized).

p. 27 "Even in the goodliest": Weir, *The Life of Elizabeth I,* p. 240.

Chapter 3

p. 31 "The greatness which he affected": Haydn, *The Portable Elizabethan Reader,* p. 389.

p. 33 "I shall require": Weir, *The Life of Elizabeth I,* pp. 23–24.

p. 34 "No prince in Europe": ibid., p. 228.

p. 35 "brother and best": ibid., p. 396.

p. 35 "When I see her": Budiansky, *Her Majesty's Spymaster,* p. 45.

p. 36 "Say to the court": Logan, *The Norton Anthology of English Literature,* p. 880.

p. 36 "I loved her": Haydn, *The Portable Elizabethan Reader,* p. 613.

p. 37 "Having this day": Logan, *The Norton Anthology of English Literature,* p. 923.

p. 38 "brought to rest" and "the world of all": ibid., p. 958.

p. 38 "immortal monuments": ibid., p. 960.

p. 38 "soul of the age": ibid., p. 1415.

p. 39 "As the dial hand": Shapiro, *A Year in the Life of William Shakespeare*, p. 74.

p. 40 "our golden knight": Editors of Time-Life, *What Life Was Like in the Realm of Elizabeth*, p. 120.

p. 40 "the master-thief": ibid., p. 121.

Chapter 4

p. 43 "She did oft ask": Pritchard, *Shakespeare's England*, p. 133.

p. 43 "To promote": Dunn, *Elizabeth and Mary*, pp. 19–20.

p. 43 "I am God's creature": ibid., p. 107.

p. 45 "First, above all": Weir, *The Life of Elizabeth I*, p. 259.

p. 46 "I do not live": ibid., p. 51.

p. 46 "continual reading": Plowden, *Tudor Women*, p. 168.

p. 47 "THENOT. ASTREA sees": "A Dialogue between two shepherds," available online at http://www.luminarium.org/renlit/thenot.htm

p. 48 "At last came": Pritchard, *Shakespeare's England*, p. 133.

p. 48 "There is a strong idea": Plowden, *Tudor Women*, p. 154.

Chapter 5

p. 51 "Boy Jack": Weir, *The Life of Elizabeth I*, p. 304.

p. 51 "I love thee": Singman, *Daily Life in Elizabethan England*, p. 39.

p. 51 "If he could get": Weir, *The Life of Elizabeth I*, pp. 18–19.

p. 52 "The heavens": Ellen Moody, "Six Elegiac Poems, Possibly by Anne Cecil de Vere, Countess of Oxford," available online at http://www.jimandellen.org/anne.cecil.poems.html (spelling modernized).

p. 53 "His judgment": Clarke, *Growing Up in Elizabethan Times*, p. 33.

p. 54 "Her memory": Plowden, *Tudor Women*, p. 123.

p. 54 "besides her perfect": ibid., p. 155.

p. 54 "children were sooner": Haydn, *The Portable Elizabethan Reader*, p. 175.

p. 54 "truth of Religion": ibid., p. 179.

p. 54 "To ride comely": Rowse, *The England of Elizabeth*, p. 531.

p. 56 "As years do grow": Ault, *Elizabethan Lyrics*, pp. 57–58.

p. 57 "How often": Plowden, *Tudor Women*, p. 129.

Chapter 6

p. 59 "After supper": Pritchard, *Shakespeare's England*, p. 138.

p. 60 "so sparkled": Dunn, *Elizabeth and Mary*, p. 29.

p. 61 "Her grace": ibid., p. 30.

p. 61 "organs, fifes": ibid., p. 33.

p. 62 "joyful ringing": Editors of Time-Life, *What Life Was Like in the Realm of Elizabeth,* p. 54.

p. 63 "so melodiously sung": Weir, *The Life of Elizabeth I,* p. 252.

p. 63 "We are frolic": Rowse, *The Elizabethan Renaissance: The Cultural Achievement,* p. 116.

p. 64 "We were admitted": Pritchard, *Shakespeare's England,* pp. 131–132.

p. 65 "Upward and downward": Rowse, *The Elizabethan Renaissance: The Cultural Achievement,* p. 117.

p. 65 "six or seven": Weir, *The Life of Elizabeth I,* p. 249.

p. 65 "When her maids": ibid., p. 230.

Chapter 7

p. 67 "Uneasy lies": Shakespeare, *Henry IV, Part 2,* act 3, scene 1.

p. 68 "I left her": Weir, *The Life of Elizabeth I,* p. 136.

p. 68 "a defect": Pritchard, *Shakespeare's England,* p. 131.

p. 69 "Where each one seeks": "Colin Clouts Come Home Againe," available online at http://darkwing.uoregon.edu/%7Erbear/colin.html

p. 70 "The doubt of future foes": Logan, *The Norton Anthology of English Literature,* p. 594.

p. 70 "any that have": Budiansky, *Her Majesty's Spymaster,* p. 138.

p. 70 "I am not unmindful": Dunn, *Elizabeth and Mary,* p. 377.

p. 71 "singed the King": Weir, *The Life of Elizabeth I,* p. 382.

p. 71 "I assure your honor": Budiansky, *Her Majesty's Spymaster,* p. 198.

p. 72 "Just look": Dunn, *Elizabeth and Mary,* p. 416.

p. 72 "The mother": Weir, *The Life of Elizabeth I,* p. 486.

INDEX

Page numbers for illustrations are in boldface

ABOUT THE AUTHOR

Kathryn Hinds grew up near Rochester, NY. In college she studied music and writing, and went on to do graduate work in comparative literature and medieval studies. She has written more than twenty-five books for young people, including the books in the series LIFE IN ANCIENT EGYPT, LIFE IN THE ROMAN EMPIRE, LIFE IN THE RENAISSANCE, and LIFE IN THE MIDDLE AGES. Kathryn lives in the north Georgia mountains with her husband, their son, and an assortment of cats and dogs. When she is not writing, she enjoys spending time with her family and friends, reading, dancing, knitting, gardening, and taking walks in the woods. Visit her online at www.kathrynhinds.com

Fox Gradin, Celestial Studios Photography